Journey Toward Intimacy
A Handbook for Lesbian Couples

Jeanne Shaw, Ph.D.
Virginia Erhardt, Ph.D.

Revised Edition

Couples Enrichment Institute
P. O. Box 420114
Atlanta, Georgia 30342-0114

Journey Toward Intimacy
A Handbook for Lesbian Couples

Jeanne Shaw, Ph.D.
Virginia Erhardt, Ph.D.

Published by:

The Couples Enrichment Institute
P.O. Box 420114
Atlanta, Georgia 30342-0114

Printed in the United States of America

ISBN 1-891257-05-6
Library of Congress Catalogue Card Number 98-92433

CONTENTS

Warning - Disclaimer

This book is meant to provide information to lesbian couples on the subject matter covered. It is sold with the understanding that the publisher and authors are not engaged in rendering professional services through this handbook. Although the handbook may be used in conjunction with therapy, it does not take the place of therapy. If counseling is required, a licensed mental health professional should be contracted.

It is not within the scope of this handbook to provide complete information on the topic. You are urged to read available material about sexual relationships and tailor the information to your needs. For more material, please see the section on Suggested Readings in the Appendix.

Every effort has been made to make this handbook concise and accurate. However, there may be mistakes, both typographical and in content. Further, standards of couples' sexual behavior change with social change; thus, some concepts basic to this handbook may shift over time.

The purpose of this handbook is to educate and inspire you toward fulfilling your human sexual potential. The authors and Couples Enrichment Institute have neither liability nor responsibility to any person or couple with respect to any loss or damage caused or alleged to have been caused, directly or indirectly, by the use of information contained herein.

If you do not wish to be bound by the above, you may return this book unused to the publisher for a full refund.

Welcome to the Handbook!

This handbook is for lesbian couples who want a lasting, juicy relationship as well as for couples who are bored or unfulfilled. You will be introduced to new perspectives about being sexually intimate and deeply related and invited to risk being erotic with your partner without help from fantasies, videos, sex toys, or genital techniques.

Most couples early in their relationship easily experience good sex; they play, lust, laugh, love, and enjoy each other. Occasionally, sex toys and erotica contribute variety to their genital repertoire. Under the influence of strong chemistry, new couples become genitally aroused and believe their initial lustiness is lifelong. However, lust does not last, for if it did, emotional and sexual growth would fade. Waning sexual energy is fertile ground for personal exploration and increased self-awareness.

Creating enduring sexual satisfaction in a lifelong relationship requires the courage, integrity, and emotional maturity to face waning sexual energy, low desire, and ambivalence. Although society will not validate your sexuality, you have the ability to validate your own natural desire for lesbian contact. Expressing yourself sexually in a long-term relationship is developmental. To understand your sexual self with your partner, to play, to be curious, to discover how familiarity dilutes sexual energy, to use the tension your differences create, and to allow differentness to recapture sexual energy in an already rewarding relationship are developmental tasks for lesbian sex.

Claiming your part in creating your relationship with good humor, good will, and respect is an effective characteristic you may already enjoy. And, for juicy sex, eroticizing physical contact while managing and soothing your own anxiety is as essential as it can be awkward.

7

These pages can guide you into new conceptual territory about self-motivation, maturity, and integrity. Couples say the exercises are rewarding, eye-opening, and somewhat nerve-racking after they agree to stop protecting each other from their real experience. The exercises are not sex manual techniques. They were originally designed for workshops with heterosexual couples. The handbook offers a workshop adventure at home without the support or expense of a vacation weekend.

There is no wrong way to approach these exercises; however, following the guidelines in sequence will soften your journey.

General Guidelines:

1. Read the suggestions at the beginning of each exercise and do the exercise.

2. Make time with your partner to compare responses.

3. Don't explode, don't cave in, and don't leave. Just quiet yourself.

4. After each discussion, talk about how it was for you to consider the topic. *This is vital.*

Good Journey!

Purposes

1. Observe how your own beliefs and attitudes affect your sexual energy.

2. Learn how knowing *yourself* further can lead to sexual enthusiasm with your partner.

3. Recognize the thoughts, feelings, and behaviors that enhance or block your sexual energy and expression.

4. Explore the significance of anxiety-reducing behaviors (safe, familiar, comfortable, friendly, cozy) and intimate behaviors (risky, unfamiliar, uncomfortable, erotic).

5. Focus on intimacy and erotic feelings during sex instead of fantasy and techniques.

6. Learn how partner-validation builds good will and self-validation builds sexual potential.

7. Recognize the difference between fusion, closeness, and intimacy.

8. Explore, in relationship, your capacity for self-development, intimacy, and eroticism.

Write or think about your responses to the following statements and then share them with your partner.

My wish for *myself* in completing this handbook:

My wish for *my partner* in completing this handbook:

My hope for *our relationship*:

I am willing to struggle with myself while I am with my partner and talk about issues I find very hard to think about, let alone discuss:

☐ Yes   ☐ No

Other comments:

Sexual Attitudes

The first exercise is a survey of your sexual attitudes. Attitudes are rarely neutral and can support or weaken your sexual desire for each other. Attitudes are formed by the beliefs and values you learn as a child and reassess as an adult. Attitudes mature as women mature. To stay connected, both obvious and subtle changes in attitude must be noticed and revealed, together and separately.

Your sexual attitudes have meaning. They affect your choices and direct your behavior. When you explore attitudes with your partner, you connect purposefully instead of accidentally, absently, resentfully, or not at all. Talking and listening is how you learn each others' sexual aspirations and fears. Developing yourself in relationship should be a deeply satisfying, if trying, experience.

Wanting to transform unsatisfactory behaviors into fulfilling experience invites your presence. Sexual intimacy requires presence, especially in the face of anxiety. Although sexual presence is a choice, it does not come naturally. A taste for sexual presence is developed over time. Fortunately, play is a natural way to develop sexual presence. Playing lets you risk being erotic instead of modest, inhibited, or fearful.

Self-awareness is the first step toward being the sexual partner you can be. Self-awareness helps you identify your attitudes. Managing your anxiety helps you respond and hear your partner's responses without overreacting, leaving, or withholding your experience. You gain integrity when good will and self-respect surmount your need for "peace at all costs." One of the greatest sacrifices of this cost is your desire for your partner.

Suggestions:

1. Fill out the Sexual Attitude Survey. Choose quickly and spontaneously. There are no wrong answers.

2. Make enough time with your partner to compare responses. Note which meanings are unique to you.

3. You learn most when you differ, not when you agree. Difference triggers uneasiness, and uneasiness opens opportunities to deepen intimacy. Agreement offers comfort. Both are necessary for a juicy relationship.

4. With each difference, either partner can ask, "How is this difference *useful* to our sexual relationship?" "How can I address my uneasiness with my partner instead of alone?"

5. Don't explode, don't cave in, and don't leave. Just quiet yourself. Continue talking until you finish or agree to continue later. Honor your agreements.

6. Afterwards, talk about what it was like to discuss your sexual attitudes.

Sexual Attitude Survey

Indicate whether you Agree or Disagree:

( ) 1. Sex is perfect, nothing needs to change (skip this question if you fell in love recently).

( ) 2. By now, my partner should be sensitive enough to know what turns me on without my saying so.

( ) 3. Sexual pleasure should be easy and spontaneous.

( ) 4. I can surprise myself with new ways to make love.

( ) 5. I tell her what pleasures me sexually and what does not.

( ) 6. At times in my life I have had sex when I really did not want to, just to please my partner.

( ) 7. I often enhance my arousal by having a sexual fantasy while having sex with my partner.

( ) 8. I wish I could ignore my partner's desire for sex, but she tries so hard to please me I feel guilty saying no.

( ) 9. I could behave more erotically if I thought my partner could handle it.

( ) 10. During sex, I can tell when my partner is connected to a fantasy instead of to me.

( ) 11. Sex for me is often monotonous.

( ) 12. I want to give my partner what she wants but I do not know what that is and neither does she.

( ) 13. I want to give my partner what she wants and I know what that is, but I just cannot do it.

( ) 14. Something is missing sexually that I cannot name.

( ) 15. I feel confident about my ability to arouse her.

( ) 16. I usually do not say how I feel when I think my partner will get upset or make me anxious.

( ) 17. I would like to explore being uninhibited with her.

( ) 18. I have faked orgasms to please my partner.

( ) 19. She should want sex or agree to it when I desire it.

( ) 20. To enjoy sex, I must first feel emotionally connected.

( ) 21. To feel emotionally connected, I must first have sex.

( ) 22. When conflict comes up, I use it to clear the air.

( ) 23. I do not need her to see every issue my way.

( ) 24. I hate responding to this questionnaire.

( ) 25. A statement I wish had been included:

Common Misinformed Beliefs about Sex

The next exercise is a brief list of common erroneous beliefs about sex. Any one of them can impede your sexual enjoyment. We encourage you to question and correct your misinformation. Most couples have differences in what they believe. Honoring these differences helps you know yourselves as separate people. Erotic sex requires you to feel autonomous and separate, before you move toward deep arousal and orgasmic connection with each other.

When you shift from being misinformed to knowledgeable, you increase your sexual possibilities. Almost everybody in our culture learns, without awareness, to think in ways that undermine natural sexuality. Learning to hide your sexual nature is part of being socialized. The very act of burying your sexual energy supports those beliefs and attitudes that destroy wholeness. Expose your beliefs effectively through gentle, respectful discussion with your partner.

You may benefit from reading a good sex education book together. Your partner will tell you if you would benefit. SIECUS, AASECT (see Community Resources, p. 109), bookstores, the internet, and the Suggested Reading section (p. 107) can locate good sex education references. Sex education and erotica are not equivalent. Good sex education informs and guides. The purpose of erotica is to arouse.

The next page is a list of common erroneous beliefs about women and sex, followed by the same list with a short commentary based on today's social beliefs and biological knowledge.

Suggestions:

1. Mark each belief in the first list as true or false, then read the commentary.

2. Make time with your partner to compare and discuss.

3. If you have major disagreements about items and one of you believes an item is completely true, decide what holding different views means to your relationship. Discuss how these differences affect you, personally.

4. Don't explode, don't cave in, and don't leave. Just quiet yourself.

5. Afterwards, talk about how it was for you to discuss your misconceptions. Was it difficult, easy, stirring, boring, enjoyable, insightful, risky?

Common Misinformed Beliefs about Sex

☐ When she is wet, she is ready.

☐ If you love each other and communicate, good sex will follow naturally.

☐ Sexual problems mean something is wrong in the relationship.

☐ Casual sex with another is more exciting than intimate sex with your partner.

☐ In a good sexual relationship, you have a fulfilling experience each time.

☐ After age 25 your sex drive decreases and then stops altogether by 60.

☐ If either partner is aroused, sex must follow or you risk disappointment.

☐ Having "G" spot and multiple orgasms means you are sexually liberated.

☐ Menopause and hysterectomy decrease sexual desire.

☐ When you lose desire, the best remedy is to find another partner.

☐ Lesbians in relationship do not masturbate.

☐ If you love your partner you should not need to use a vibrator.

☐ Sex should always be gentle and nurturing.

- [ ] Both partners must have high desire for sex to take place or be enjoyable.

- [ ] Sexual give and take is always equal and reciprocal.

- [ ] The best orgasm is with your eyes closed, having a sexual fantasy.

- [ ] Limerance (mindless bliss!) is destined to disappear and there is nothing you can do to stop it.

- [ ] When you feel affectionate and companionable, do not rock the boat.

- [ ] If you cannot make her come, or if you do not come, you are sexually inadequate or not performing well.

Commentary on Common Misinformed Beliefs

WHEN SHE IS WET, SHE IS READY. Not necessarily. Some women get wet before they have any awareness of arousal, and others feel arousal without lubricating.

IF YOU LOVE EACH OTHER AND COMMUNICATE, GOOD SEX WILL FOLLOW NATURALLY. Not for most. Communication is necessary but not sufficient for erotic sex. Erotic energy with a long-term partner is developed over time with that partner. A truer statement is, "Maturity, integrity, emotional freedom, and sexual skills promote erotic sex."

SEXUAL PROBLEMS MEAN SOMETHING IS WRONG IN THE RELATIONSHIP. More often, sexual problems mean a relationship is ripe for change and growth. A sexual problem can be a personal statement expressed physically that pushes partners to develop further. Couples can have good sex even if something is wrong.

CASUAL SEX WITH ANOTHER IS MORE EXCITING THAN INTIMATE SEX WITH YOUR PARTNER. When individuals are not emotionally involved, sexual excitement is more tolerable. Casual sex eventually gets boring, but nothing is more exciting or anxiety producing than erotic sex between life partners.

IN A GOOD SEXUAL RELATIONSHIP YOU HAVE A FULFILLING EXPERIENCE EACH TIME. No, you don't. Everything has cycles, including sex. Sex will be tepid, mind-blowing, monotonous, awful, delightful, adequate, and stunning, depending on mental, physical, emotional, and environmental variables. (The longer partners are together, the more variables; the wonder is how anybody ever has a fulfilling experience.)

AFTER AGE 25 YOUR SEX DRIVE DECREASES AND STOPS ALTOGETHER BY 60. Not true, especially not for older women, whose skill and personal confidence increase with age.

IF EITHER PARTNER IS AROUSED, SEX MUST FOLLOW OR YOU RISK DISAPPOINTMENT. Arousal is to be enjoyed by itself. It can be joined or observed, as partners decide how they want to express themselves sexually. Disappointment is manageable.

HAVING "G" SPOT AND MULTIPLE ORGASMS MEANS YOU ARE SEXUALLY LIBERATED. Only if being liberated means you are free to experience bodily pleasures with your partner. Women can learn how to stimulate each others' Graffenburg spot (see Suggested Reading).

MENOPAUSE AND HYSTERECTOMY DECREASE SEXUAL DESIRE AND AROUSAL. Hysterectomy does not physically affect desire or arousal. Decreasing estrogen levels can raise, lower, or have no effect on desire and arousal. Some menopausal women over-lubricate; others dry up.

WHEN YOU LOSE SEXUAL DESIRE, THE BEST REMEDY IS TO FIND ANOTHER PARTNER. This remedy maintains the myth that somebody else is responsible for your sexual potential. The best remedy is to sexualize and liberate yourself in this relationship.

LESBIANS IN RELATIONSHIP DO NOT MASTURBATE. Of course they do. They just do not often discuss it. Masturbation is not a substitute for partner sex, it is sex-for-one. Include her anytime!

IF YOU LOVE YOUR PARTNER YOU SHOULD NOT NEED TO USE A VIBRATOR. Love is not the issue. If manual or oral stimulation is not enough to reach your personal orgasm threshold, occasional vibrator use can help. You will not fall in love with your vibrator.

SEX SHOULD ALWAYS BE GENTLE AND NURTURING. Sex should be any way that feels good: gentle, primitive, lusty, even rough if it suits both partners. Nurturance is nice but not sexual.

BOTH PARTNERS MUST HAVE HIGH DESIRE FOR SEX TO OCCUR OR BE ENJOYABLE. Ideal, but rare. One partner should have enough desire to invite the other's participation. Desire can be as simple as being willing to participate and not as a duty or obligation.

SEXUAL GIVE AND TAKE IS ALWAYS EQUAL AND RECIPROCAL. Give and take is individual, not reciprocal. You give because you enjoy "doing" your partner, but giving can also mean letting your partner "do" you. If you give only to get, your partner is eventually going to feel used.

THE BEST ORGASM IS WITH EYES CLOSED AND A SEXUAL FANTASY. That is an orgasm with a connection to your fantasy, not your partner. The best orgasm is with your eyes open, literally or metaphorically connected to your partner.

LIMERANCE IS DESTINED TO DISAPPEAR AND THERE IS NOTHING YOU CAN DO ABOUT IT. When initial feelings of mindless bliss wane, comfort and familiarity take over. What you can do about it is open yourself to discomfort and strangeness. Use (instead of avoid) conflict and differences. The unfamiliar fosters erotic sex.

WHEN YOU FEEL AFFECTIONATE AND COMPANION-ABLE, DO NOT ROCK THE BOAT. Affection is comfortable, familiar, and necessary. Intimate energy is unfamiliar and uncomfortable. If you are willing to have sexual excitement in your relationship, dig out your strange, wise, intimate, primitive "Dirty Goddess" energy.

LOW SEXUAL DESIRE AND INFREQUENT SEX LEADS TO AFFAIRS, BREAKUPS, OR BOREDOM. It can. But not when you are willing to risk being your Dirty Goddess self. Dirty Goddess abhors stagnation and boredom and therefore prohibits them in herself.

IF YOU CANNOT "MAKE HER" COME YOU'RE NOT PER-FORMING WELL. She is responsible for her orgasms. Co-operate and respect your desires and hers. Share thoughts and feelings, but not genitals. Thinking about your performance prevents your emotional presence. This is a turn-off. Enjoy how delicious she is, "do" her for your own enjoyment, not as an obligation.

Wake-Up Calls

Couples leave a trail of wake-up calls to let each other know something is percolating that needs to change. This happens often when you hesitate about sex and feel uncomfortable or defensive when you discuss sexual issues. Everybody has effective and ineffective ways to respond to wake-up calls; however, we are sometimes unaware or do not want to know when our attempts are ineffective.

Wake-up calls invite change. Ignored, they become self-defeating and repetitive. Objectionable behavior does not go away by itself no matter how long you ignore it. Listen for whispering wake-up calls lest they escalate into painful betrayals, defensiveness, nastiness, and absence.

A wake-up call is subtle or obvious tension in yourself or feedback from your partner. It alerts you to a need for change, usually about something you are avoiding. Your responses reveal your level of perception and willingness to engage effectively. Engaging yourself about this will almost always feel discomforting. Does your relationship encourage this depth of personal growth? Do you tell your partner habits you wish you did not have, and deal with them? Is your relationship merely a convenient place for money-meal-company-laundry-reassurance?

Talking about uncomfortable issues can transform wake-up calls into personal insights, energy, and increasing willingness to explore being downright genitally connected.

There are too many variations of wake-up calls to list here, and they happen differently in every relationship. How you manage yourself in the face of anxiety can keep you ignorant or open your eyes. For more information read the books, *Why Marriages Succeed or Fail* and *Permanent Partners* (see Suggested Readings, p. 107).

23

Suggestions:

1. Mark each characteristic that fits you.

2. Check each characteristic you see in your partner.

3. Compare and discuss responses. Note how quickly or reluctantly you make a rebuttal or agreement.

4. When your partner is brave and honest enough to reveal herself, note how you receive the information.

5. Don't explode, don't cave in, and don't leave. Just quiet yourself. No, we are not having fun, yet.

6. Afterwards, talk about what it was like to discuss your wake-up call revelations.

Wake-Up Calls

Avoiding Contact

☐ No time for each other.

☐ No affectionate or sexual touch.

☐ No playing, alone or together.

☐ Doing more projects alone than together, and one partner is dissatisfied with this arrangement.

☐ Longing for (or ignoring) a sexual connection with your partner while you fill time with someone else.

☐ No relaxation, insights, or self-disclosure.

☐ Watching TV, going online, being alone with hobbies, avoiding contact.

☐ Sex is a bore, a chore, anxious, or nonexistent.

☐ Too shy, afraid, inhibited to approach her.

Ineffective Contact

☐ Becoming distant or aloof.

☐ Keeping a painful, lonely secret.

☐ Being argumentative, defensive, critical.

☐ Excusing defensiveness by impulsive arguing and knee-jerk reacting.

☐ Attacking as a way to relate when you feel stressed, hurt, angry, disappointed, frustrated.

☐ Blaming, shaming, putting down yourself or her.

☐ Tolerating blame, shame, and put-downs.

☐ Escalating negativity.

☐ Giving or receiving the silent treatment.

☐ Ignoring what needs to change.

☐ Accepting passivity, being passive.

☐ Withdrawing into isolation, sulking, complaining, threatening, or whining.

☐ Feeling helpless.

☐ Depending on her to initiate contact.

Loss of Integrity

☐ Being dishonest, then excusing yourself.

☐ Lying to yourself.

☐ Hiding from your own rejection or her rejection.

☐ Saying you agree when you do not, to keep harmony.

☐ Accepting her as dutiful instead of willing.

☐ Overworking, overeating, overspending, gambling, drug abuse, any over-behaviors that hurt you or her.

☐ Being silent or contributing to her overbehaviors. (You are not responsible for her behavior, but you do have a part in maintaining it.)

☐ Hiding porn, masturbating in secret, retreating from sexual contact with her, or secrecy around non-exclusivity while you both avoid the issue.

☐ Tolerating physical and emotional absence.

☐ Exploding, caving in, spacing out, numbing, leaving, as a habitual pattern.

☐ Tolerating her exploding, caving in, etc., without effective discussion.

Insufficient Good Will

☐ Expressing or feeling contempt for your partner.

☐ Tolerating contempt instead of dealing with it.

☐ Being sarcastic, scathing, nasty, or mean.

☐ Tolerating sarcasm, scathing, nastiness, or meanness.

☐ Lying.

☐ Hostile teasing.

☐ Slapping, hitting, pinching, pushing, kicking, or any hurtful physical expression, accidental or on purpose.

☐ Punishment of any kind.

☐ Expressing anger in a way that violates or demeans your partner or yourself physically, mentally, emotionally, spiritually, and any other way.

☐ Tolerating harmful expressions as though you had no adult voice or choice.

Hints for Respecting Your Wake-Up Calls:

Accept your own and her right to disagree.

Be separate and different in a working relationship.

You can ask for change of behavior, not of experience (experience is not negotiable).

Realize that neither of you is innocent, no matter who does what to whom.

Focus on your own experience so you do not get caught up in manipulation, yours or hers.

Experiencing lack of control over your or her habitual, automatic, negative reactions does not excuse you from your responsibility to contain yourself.

Behave toward your partner with kindness and compassion, especially when that feels impossible.

Do this especially when she does not cooperate.

Choose integrity, self-respect, and good will over comfort and security whenever you have a choice.

Tolerate your partner's growth.

Define these concepts together so you can visualize what they look like in action.

Notes

Characteristics of Sexually Alive Couples

Satisfied, sexually alive, lifelong lesbian couples have described for us the relationship qualities that make their partnerships enviable. We share them with you in the next exercise so that you can weigh your own strengths and positive qualities against known success.

The developmental quality of emotional maturity is a monumental task and basic requirement for erotic sex. Thus, your level of maturity is a starting place. A definition is spelled out in another exercise, but repeated here:

• Define yourself with your partner.
• Soothe your own anxiety.
• Be ready to admit you are wrong.
• Validate and support your own feelings.
• Manage your own insecurity, anxiety, and conflict.
• Observe and regulate your own responses.
• Stay emotionally connected to your partner.
• Verify yourself as whole and separate.
• All without exploding, caving in, or leaving.

Clarify the characteristics of being sexually alive in your own mind and then with your partner. Consider which qualities are your present strengths and which you want to enhance. Think what a healthy balance of separateness and togetherness looks like for the two of you, and how a celebration of differentness might encourage erotic sex.

Ideally, sexually alive couples speak their truth with compassion. They trust themselves and their partners to manage and share hurt, anger, and other tough feelings. They give each other room to grow, tolerate the results of that growth, and then go around *shamelessly* enjoying and relishing each other mentally, emotionally, and physically. It feels good to be in their company even when they disagree.

31

Suggestions:

1. Allow plenty of time to discuss the qualities of sexually alive couples.

2. Consider how each quality on the list is, or is not yet, part of your own relationship.

3. If you think you are in a dead relationship, consider your part in creating it.

4. Don't explode, don't cave in, and don't leave. Just quiet yourself. Focus on yourself, not her. Change is most negotiable when negotiating with yourself.

5. Take time to discuss what it was like for you to talk about the qualities that keep (or might keep) your relationship alive and juicy.

Characteristics of Sexually Alive Couples

☐ Sense of humor.

☐ More joy, play, and laughter than regret or resentment.

☐ Respect for yourself and your partner.

☐ Frequent affectionate and sexual touch.

☐ Predictability, comfort, familiarity (Closeness).

☐ Unpredictability, anxiety, newness (Intimacy).

☐ Presence, being fully contactable and responsible.

☐ Emotional separateness and togetherness.

☐ Ability for self-validation, self-awareness, self-soothing, self-monitoring, autonomy (Maturity).

☐ Bringing your own wholeness (Integrity) to relationship.

I want:

Here's how I might get it:

I wish my partner had more:

Productive Disclosure

One of the more difficult conversations for partners is the one in which they tell, or don't tell, what is happening sexually, especially when they feel frustrated or disappointed. "I don't want to hurt you." "I don't want to push you away." "I dread your reaction." "It isn't your fault." Partners protect each other from the reality of their feelings, for example, by silence, unending power struggles, and cheerful, impersonal conversations about non-threatening topics.

Talking personally about your real experience eliminates emotional walls while generating *productive anxiety*. Productive anxiety mobilizes you to speak your truth. For example, facing your partner and speaking up for yourself without her support can be nerve-wracking. When you are used to leaning on your partner and you stand on your own, you may feel scared and she may feel rejected, irritated, afraid, relieved, or appreciative. You cheat her when you protect her from your feelings. On the other hand, you cheat yourself when you impulsively spill feelings without monitoring yourself, as if you were not in charge of your own choice and style of expression.

Making an agreement with yourself to say your piece with compassion goes a long way toward boosting self-respect. Self-respect helps you focus on your own experience instead of the faults, deficiencies, and oversights of your partner. To speak the unspeakable without blaming or shaming is vital to erotic sex. When she speaks, you hear her without feeling devastated or getting your feelings bruised. In any case, emotional bruises heal quickly when you are an adult in charge of yourself.

You are competent to understand you are getting or giving a gift of knowing whether or not you elect to apply it. Sexual intimacy cannot advance without verbal, physical, and emotional contact.

You walk in integrity when you are fully yourself with your partner, open to her and yourself. Intimacy, like integrity, can be unilateral. One can feel it without the other feeling the same way, but when partners experience intimacy simultaneously, that is special!

Suggestions:

1. Fill out the Disclosure Checklist by yourself.

2. Make time to be with your partner to compare and discuss what each has written.

3. Don't explode, don't cave in, and don't leave. Just quiet yourself.

4. When you have talked as much as you are going to, discuss how talking about disclosure was for you.

Productive Disclosure

1. When I feel anxious about being sexual with you, I:

2. Sometimes your touch feels _____, and I:

3. I'm supposed to like everything we do sexually, but:

4. I truly love how you touch me when you:

5. I feel something special during sex when:

6. When I feel "careful" during sex, I:

7. I wish I would change how I:

8. If you could enjoy me more, I might:

9. If I could enjoy myself more, I might:

10. If I could enjoy you more, I might:

11. I think I would turn on intensely if I:

12. Sex is only _____ right now; I want:

13. What I want from you outside of bed is:

14. I know when your body is with me and your spirit is somewhere else, by:

15. At times, I could get primitive and lusty, like:

16. I am afraid you will/will not tell me if you dislike something sexually, and:

17. If I tell you I dislike something, you might:

18. Sex is/is not fun for me, and:

19. I sometimes pretend to have an orgasm so that:

20. When I get the nerve, I will talk about:

Sexual Scripts

Each of us learns as a child how to behave in order to be acceptable to families, peers, and society. Women receive important positive and negative nonverbal and spoken messages about how to think, feel, and behave according to the social measures of the day. Parents, teachers, and other adults impose rules on young minds. Messages of sexuality and its traditional status as taboo and unclean tend to confuse or mislead us. Often, unspoken directives tell us unmistakably which topics and behaviors are off limits. And, in spite of all this, children develop sexually.

Children get "sexual scripts," hidden prescriptions for how to be and how not to be (hetero) sexual. Then, they grow up with behavior that seems prescribed, clueless that their scripts obstruct sexual intimacy. Raising childhood scripts from subconscious to conscious awareness allows you the choice to keep what is constructive and discard the rest. The subconscious mind draws upon scripts for survival.

Uncovering your particular script and using that information on behalf of personal development is a lifelong, adult task. Scripts, by definition hidden from consciousness, are uncovered through such mental detective work as attention to your behavior, thoughts, and feelings, and bridging your present feelings to attitudes, hurts, and joys from childhood. When you can acknowledge the old prescriptions, you have the option to change them to fit you now or dispense with them. Self-observation and the resulting increase in awareness expand your options for living as a sexual being.

The next exercise can help you observe your script. If you find a blind spot, ask your partner for help, guess, or make up a response. If you do not know what ideas and values you received from parents or surrogate parents, think about your present values. Did they come from parental figures or playmates, sitters, teachers? Are they the result of acceptance or resistance to the rules imposed on you?

Suggestions:

1. Privately, write or ponder your responses to the Sexual Script items.

2. Make enough time to discuss both sets of responses. This information, while not secret, is private, so respect your partner's disclosures. Listen attentively without trying to fix her or give advice.

3. Don't explode, don't cave in, and don't leave. Just quiet yourself.

4. When you have shared as much as you're going to, discuss how talking about sexual scripts felt to you.

Sexual Script

1. Write a positive idea you received from your mother
   (or mother surrogate) about sex:

2. Write a positive idea you received from your father
   (or father surrogate) about sex:

3. Write a negative idea you received from your mother
   (or mother surrogate) about sex:

4. Write a negative idea you received from your father
   (or father surrogate) about sex:

5. How do your script messages affect your sexual behavior *now*?

6. If you could change anything about your present sexual experience, how do you imagine behaving?

7. What would you like your children (your partner, other loved ones) to learn about sex?

Internalized Homophobia and Your Script

Just as people are given messages beginning in childhood about life in general and sex in particular, you are also taught attitudes about differentness. Even if people mean to take pride in ways in which they are different from the mainstream, early script messages and social disapproval remain lodged in the subconscious mind.

An unacknowledged rule of silence is set by parents who, for whatever reason, never speak of, or ask questions about, their children's sexual feelings or orientation. When these children grow up to be gay, they believe they are supposed to keep silent about whom they love. Beyond this "no-talk" rule, is the pervasive atmosphere of negativity about being gay that we find in most homes, religions, and society as a whole.

Homophobia is the fear, loathing, or avoidance of gay people. Internalized homophobia is the fear, shame, and self-hatred that lurks in (or out of) gay people's awareness. It is this unconscious attitude that keeps a lesbian from using the correct pronoun in reference to her partner, even if nothing concrete is at stake. It is this unrecognized bias that in subtle and insidious ways keeps lesbians and gay men from challenging heterosexism (the assumption straight people make that everyone around them is heterosexual and that heterosexuality is superior to homosexuality).

Female sexuality has traditionally been a story of unactualized or thwarted potential. Few women in our culture reach adulthood without a burden of guilt, shame, or repression that limits sexual pleasure. This burden is heavy for lesbians and often creates difficulty, particularly when the passion of early relationship has diminished. Societal and internalized homophobia foster complicated and often homophobic scripts for lesbians.

The next exercise can help you uncover internalized homophobia. More than women in general, you will find that your sexual script is from the wrong drama and must be revised to fit you.

Suggestions:

1. Individually write or ponder your responses to the eight Internalized Homophobia items.

2. Make enough time to discuss both sets of responses. This is vulnerable information. Listen compassionately without trying to fix your partner.

3. Don't explode, don't cave in, and don't leave. Just quiet yourself.

4. When you have shared as much as you are going to, discuss what talking about internalized homophobia was like for you.

Internalized Homophobia

1. Write positive and negative ideas you received from parental figures about being lesbian.

2. Write positive and negative ideas you received from religion, teachers, and peers about being lesbian.

3. How do these messages affect how you feel about yourself and your sexual experience, now?

4. Write or discuss everything you can think of that feels good to you about being a lesbian and having people know you are a lesbian.

5. Write or discuss whatever you can think of that feels uncomfortable about being a lesbian and having people know you are a lesbian.

6. As honestly as possible, note which of the items you generated (in #5 above) come from inside you rather than from actual concerns about discrimination and survival.

7. Imagine you are out shopping. wearing a bright purple tee shirt that says on the front and back in huge, red letters, I AM A LESBIAN. How might you feel?

8. If you could change anything about being lesbian, what would you change and how do you imagine your life might be different, as a result?

Notes

Perspectives on Sex

Each generation has its own unique perspective on sex and its accompanying knowledge, skills, behavior, and experience. Religions have guidelines, communities have rules, families have power, and peers have information, real and imaginary. No wonder we grow up confused about sex, especially when a felt orientation does not fit the teachings of church, community, family, or peers. In the next exercise, you have an opportunity to uncover more about your broader, social beliefs and attitudes about sex.

Perspectives are presented here in two categories: conventional, meaning customary and standard, and unconventional, meaning uncommon or unique. Conventional perspectives focus on romantic notions of dependency and security. Conventional notions imply that sex is an appetite like hunger. If you are not sexually "hungry" after some period of sexual abstinence, you are labelled "sexually anorexic" instead of "overcome by integrity." Western culture fosters romance: "You and I are together against a homophobic world," and dependency: "Love me and take care of me, then I will never leave you, and in the bargain I promise not to grow up." Behaving as a parent or child with your partner decreases sexual desire because leaning and controlling invite dependency, not erotic love. Believing you cannot be different or separate from your partner creates protective, not erotic feelings.

The unconventional perspective is based on maturity, self-respect, integrity, and the idea that good sex happens with fullness, not neediness. In all aspects of the media, mature love is unconventional, and until recently, lesbian love was unmentionable. With a clear intent to stick together as best friends, and yet be separate individuals, you can create a juicy sex life. A mature woman soothes herself instead of demanding her partner comfort her. She does not need her partner, she wants her. Paradoxically, self-sufficiency and autonomy helps partners bond *more* deeply and erotically, not less. Integrity and individuality are lasting and profoundly effective aphrodisiacs.

Suggestions:

1. Find time to do this exercise together and discuss what each item means to you. Items in both lists will fit.

2. As you discuss each concept, note how similar or different your thoughts are, whether you soothe yourself, manage anxiety, and monitor your reactions.

3. Don't explode, don't cave in, and don't leave. Just quiet yourself.

4. When you have shared as much as you are going to for now, take a few more minutes to discuss what talking about your different sexual perspectives was like.

Perspectives on Sex

Conventional Viewpoint

☐ Sex is a natural hunger.

☐ Focus is genitals, techniques, positions.

☐ Tune in to fantasy instead of your partner.

☐ Desire is a function of need.

☐ For good sex, reduce anxiety, relax, be comfortable.

☐ Orgasms are pleasant, with low level arousal.

☐ Keep silence about sexual problems. Avoid or fix.

☐ Partners validate, assure, and protect each other.

☐ Security depends on partner's behavior and mood.

☐ Emotional security overrides integrity and honesty.

☐ The main complaint is, "I am not getting what I want from my partner in this relationship."

Unconventional Viewpoint

- [ ] Good sex happens with fullness, not need.

- [ ] Focus is on intimate connection with erotic arousal.

- [ ] Tune in partner, tune in erotic arousal, no fantasy needed.

- [ ] Desire happens before, during, and after sex, a function of want, not need.

- [ ] Tolerate and manage the anxiety of intense arousal.

- [ ] Orgasms often occur with profound, erotic arousal and high intensity.

- [ ] Talking over problems is common; considered fertile ground for growth.

- [ ] Each partner validates and reassures self, creates own safety.

- [ ] Security depends on awareness, self-soothing, self-respect, and self-validation.

- [ ] Emotional security is a result of self-responsibility.

- [ ] The main complaint is, "I am not getting what I want from myself in this relationship."

Conversations about Sex

Do you remember a time early in your relationship when you talked for hours, told each other everything, and believed you would always be self-revealing and lusty? That state of mindless bliss is "limerance," when you believe your love for each other will magically erase every obstacle.

When you grew to know each other better, maturity allowed you to stay connected as you encountered disappointment, disillusion, and frustration. Had you stayed ecstatic with each other, you would not have developed into sexually mature people. The reward of discontent is creating room for growth. Instead of trying to whip your partner into shape, you accept the task of improving yourself. Communication is not the issue; you did not forget how. The issue is that neither wants to hear the other threaten the status quo and have to deal with the inevitable anxiety.

Even couples who communicate with ease and skill do not necessarily talk effectively about sex or what their hesitation means. Or what sex means, for that matter. Couples may focus on finances, work, or children, to the exclusion of more delicate topics, of which sex is probably the most complex.

Books specific to lesbian sex may help you understand your own sexual nature and, therefore, talk in greater detail about sexual issues, desires, and values. See Suggested Readings (p. 107).

The next exercise can help you re-experience each other through guided conversations about sex. You can have similar conversations about other issues by substituting money, children, whatever, for sex. Managing an awkward conversation is great practice for boosting sexual energy.

Suggestions:

1. Make time to be together to do this exercise. Write your responses or discuss while you read.

2. Take turns talking about each statement. Note how this feels: easy, difficult, fun, boring, nostalgic, sad, irritating, scary, etc.

3. Don't explode, don't cave in, and don't leave. Just quiet yourself.

4. When you have finished discussing your responses, review what you noticed happening in yourself while you engaged in conversations about sex.

Conversations about Sex

1. What I appreciate you for sexually is...

2. One of the qualities I love most about you is...

3. I chuckle when I think about...

4. A tender moment with you, sexually, was...

5. One tough time for me sexually was/is:

6. What I learned from that about myself...

7. If I had a year left to live, what I would want...

8. If you had a year left to live, what I would want...

9. I depend on you for...

10. Three ways I can think of to be together, now, that we both might enjoy are...

11. When we first got together sexually, I hoped...

12. Now my hope for the future is...

13. I feel most open and willing to have a sexually revealing conversation with you when I...

14. What I feel (think/want) sexually now, today, is...

Dysfunctional Sex, Functional Sex, and Erotic Sex

The medical view of sexual behavior offers two categories: dysfunctional and functional. This refers to plumbing, not loving. Using only two measures to evaluate sexual behavior ignores intimate sex, the deeply erotic love *experience* between life partners.

Intimate, erotic sex happens between mature partners who want and can tolerate more than functional, adequate, or boring sex. Although they may use erotica and sex toys for occasional variety, they don't attempt to juice up their sexual experience with erotica or fantasies. They, too, get boring over time. Instead, mature partners develop themselves emotionally, even though anxiety comes with the discussion or behavior. Dealing with productive anxiety in a way that serves you helps avoid dull life and sex.

What kind of sex is not eventually monotonous? The kind that fills your heart simultaneously with joy and fear, your body with desire and anxiety, your mind with anticipation and uneasiness. This sex is the result of managing real and imaginary fears, for example, of loss and impermanence, which is real; performance and approval, which is imaginary; and rejection and shame, which are past burdens carried into the present. Through self-observation and self-determination, gaining and bringing new aspects of yourself into your relationship makes for sex (and life) that is rarely monotonous. Sex does not become monotonous when you rekindle or generate your own passion for living. With this rekindling, nothing, including sex, is boring.

You and your partner probably already know how to be affectionate and close without feeling anxious. To feel erotic energy, however, means you can hold on to yourself in the face of anxiety. This requires emotional maturity. What makes erotic contact a consequence of emotional maturity? The same thing that fans your enthusiasm for anything else: mastery of the task and willingness to embrace differentness, change, and growth in the face of unease.

Suggestions:

1. Make time to do this exercise together. Read aloud, compare responses, and discuss each statement. For more information, read *Passionate Marriage*. (See Suggested Readings, p. 107).

2. The information you glean from this exercise will separate your mature from your dependent self. As a competent adult, you can speak the truth about your experience compassionately, and hear the truth, either graciously or begrudgingly, your choice.

3. Don't explode, don't cave in, and don't leave. Just quiet yourself.

4. When you have finished the exercise, discuss how you felt talking about the differences between dysfunctional, functional, and erotic sex.

Which statements fit your relationship?

Dysfunctional Sex:

☐ Chemistry is completely missing.

☐ Arousal is incomplete, absent, or fantasy-dependent.

☐ Orgasms are absent, puny, or fantasy-dependent.

☐ Physical response is insufficient.

☐ Desire for partner is low to none.

☐ Partners are disillusioned or disinterested in the problem.

☐ One of the partners carries the problem.

☐ A sexual problem maintains stability.

☐ Both ignore or misinterpret signals for change.

☐ Sexual energy threatens emotional security.

☐ Anxiety is not tolerated for any reason.

☐ Each partner wants the other to provide comfort and protection from anxiety.

Functional Sex:

☐ Chemistry is boring or mediocre except on vacation.

☐ Arousal is utilitarian, obligatory, or fantasy dependent.

☐ Orgasms are relaxing, occur at low levels of arousal.

☐ Physical response works, but without passion.

☐ Desire is utilitarian, for release.

☐ Partners can take it or leave it.

☐ No problem is noticed, just boredom.

☐ Comfort maintains the status quo.

☐ Neither risks consequences of change.

☐ Sexual energy is confined to special events and vacations

☐ Anxiety is not well tolerated.

☐ Each comforts the other to avoid anxiety.

Erotic Sex:

- [ ] Chemistry is present and changing.

- [ ] Arousal is often erotic, rarely mediocre or dull.

- [ ] Orgasms are intense, with high arousal.

- [ ] Physical response is intact.

- [ ] Desire is for partner, not for release.

- [ ] Partners increasingly interest each other.

- [ ] Problems have meaning and spur growth.

- [ ] Discomfort shifts the status quo.

- [ ] Both appreciate, tolerate, and accept change.

- [ ] Sexual energy is liberated as partners mature.

- [ ] Anxiety is managed and used for growth.

- [ ] Each soothes her own anxiety and tolerates the other's.

Notes

Closeness and Intimacy

Women thrive on closeness. People who are best friends turned on to each other sexually make excellent partners. Best friends care about and know each other so well that they can often predict one another's thoughts, feelings, and behaviors. This makes for a familiar, comfortable, stable, and affectionate partnership. A flourishing sexual relationship contains very large quantities of closeness, friendship, and comfort.

Intimacy is different from closeness. Intimacy is not very comfortable because each moment brings discomforting, new, and unpredictable inner experience. To people uneasy with the unknown, intimacy feels risky. To risk the unknown, you must first have a sense of who you are under pressure, and a certainty that you will not lose this sense of self even if (when) you merge sexually with your partner.

Unfamiliarity and differentness help solidify sexual energy when you are clear about who you are. Being deeply in touch with your separateness allows you to merge momentarily into sexual arousal and orgasm without fear that you will be consumed by your partner or your own lust. This new perspective, being separate at the same time you bond with the woman you love, while she, at that moment, is new and unpredictable, makes for erotic sexual contact.

The nature of intimacy keeps you new *to yourself*. While closeness allows you to know your partner better, intimacy allows you to know yourself better. Knowing yourself is a lifelong, dependable aphrodisiac.

We often confuse closeness with intimacy. Understanding this basic yet complicated difference can increase your experience of familiarity, comfort, and predictability, and deepen your tolerance for strangeness, discomfort, and unpredictability. Both are necessary to a lively sexual relationship. Most women know how to be close with their partner. The challenge is to be intimate and intense.

Think about how you feel when you feel erotic. Are you profoundly connected to yourself? Is that when you feel the most intensity toward your partner? Mature couples can move back and forth between closeness and intimacy, that is, between feeling safely private and being known, between comfort and anxiety, between appreciating the predictable and accepting the unknown. It is difficult to know and be known sexually and intimately at the same moment. Great effort is required to put love and sex together.

Suggestions:

1. Read the next page together until you grasp the shift in viewpoints. Discuss how each fits for you. For more information, read the *Art of Intimacy* or *Windows of Experience* (see Suggested Readings, p. 107).

2. Don't blow up, don't cave in, and don't leave. Just quiet yourself.

3. Talk about what it was like to consider how closeness and intimacy differ in your relationship.

Closeness is...

- Familiar, comfortable, and predictable.

- Affirming and sustaining your partner.

- Partners validating each other.

- When your primary awareness is your partner's thoughts and feelings.

- When your partner is slightly more important to you than you are to yourself.

- Experiencing your partner in shared space.

- Intense interpersonal awareness of your relationship to your partner.

- Caring for and complementing each other.

- Gladly giving up portions of personal space and options so you can know her more deeply.

- Necessarily negotiable because it involves behavior.

- Knowing your partner.

Intimacy is...

- Unfamiliar, uncomfortable, unpredictable, unsure.

- Affirming and sustaining yourself.

- Self-validating, self-soothing, self-supportive.

- Being fully yourself without stopping her from being fully herself.

- Relinquishing no part of yourself to bond with her.

- Experiencing yourself fully when you are with her.

- Intense personal awareness of your relationship to yourself, with her.

- Being willing to manage your anxiety and tolerate hers.

- Being willing to change some of your perspectives in the service of your growth, not her insecurities.

- Choosing to be simultaneously truthful, compassionate, and related.

- Not negotiable because it involves experience and experience is never negotiable.

- Knowing yourself.

Balancing Togetherness and Individuality

This exercise is meant to increase your awareness of intimacy and enliven your erotic connection. Intimacy includes:

• The ability and willingness to know yourself and let your partner know you.

• Accepting your partner as she is.

• Supporting yourself via self-validation and self-soothing while you risk self-disclosure.

• Tolerating her anxiety and soothing your own while you are being deeply, authentically yourself with her.

• Fostering this bold way to relate through self-respect and self-empowerment.

You can see that the characteristics of intimacy and maturity overlap. Intimacy requires togetherness and individuality at the same time. This can be difficult in lesbian relationships. Being lesbian does not create the difficulty; the issue is in the way all women are socialized. We celebrate women's natural capacity to relate in close and mutually empathic ways. Yet, we lament individuality forfeited and fusion elicited when focus is exclusively on comfort and harmony.

Because fusion prohibits having separate thoughts, feelings, behavior, or personal boundaries, it deadens sexual energy. Couples can become so close and so much alike that neither partner is separate enough to create sexual tension. Attraction for "other" assumes the "other" is separate from yourself. Without separate identities, sex with your partner begins to seem like contact with another you. Sex, then, is no longer the ecstatic experience of two separate people coming together, the union when personal boundaries are temporarily obliterated in arousal and orgasm, but a self-self too familiar contact. The sexual "urge to merge" arises *after* partners experience individual emotional separateness.

Fusion robs both partners of identity. Ambivalence about forfeited identity is expressed in various ways such as creating distance through conflict, secret affairs, break-ups, unsatisfactory serial exclusivity. When emotionally fused partners maintain a relationship over time, one or both partners usually begin to avoid sexual contact.

The next exercises differentiate between Individuality and Distance, Togetherness and Fusion.

Suggestions:

1. Circle each item that fits you or your relationship.

2. Compare where individuality fades and distance grows. Do the same for togetherness and fusion.

3. Don't explode, don't cave in, and don't leave. Just quiet yourself.

4. Afterwards, talk about what it was like to discuss where your relationship fits on the Individuality-Distance and Togetherness-Fusion dimensions.

Individuality and Distance

1. I define my own identity as distinct and different from that of my partner.

2. I see myself as an independent entity with individual beliefs, goals, and boundaries.

3. My behavior is usually autonomous; I am responsibly self-governing and self-reliant.

4. I am able to decline irrelevant or inappropriate "shoulds" from my partner.

5. My personal boundaries and identity are not negotiable.

6. I consider input from my partner and then make my choices.

7. I enjoy my relationship, but I do not need it to complete myself.

8. In this relationship, we often do not communicate effectively.

9. When we do communicate, it is usually superficial.

10. I have difficulty disclosing my internal self to my partner.

11. I find it necessary to maintain a "strong" or "perfect" facade with my partner.

12. I have trouble asking my partner for anything.

13. There seems to be no interpersonal intensity or tension in our relationship.

14. One or both of us takes refuge in work, jobs with travel, or activities apart.

15. I often need to be authoritarian and dogmatic about boundaries in my relationship.

16. I tend to reject suggestions and ideas from my partner without really listening.

Togetherness and Fusion

1. I feel drawn to my partner.

2. I enjoy our mutual interest in, and involvement with, each other.

3. My partner and I are quite considerate of and responsive to each other.

4. I enjoy companionship and closeness with her.

5. I experience our relationship as mutually supportive.

6. I am open to hearing and willing to learn from my partner's perspective.

7. I enjoy the degree of comfort and harmony in our relationship.

8. I appreciate our ability to tolerate the anxiety of constructive conflict and exploring our differences.

9. My partner and I have become cautious with each other.

10. Being careful seems necessary to protect our comfort, harmony, and compatibility.

11. I am afraid the ways in which we are different might threaten our relationship.

12. We try always to agree.

13. I need my partner's approval.

14. I do not feel safe letting my partner know me well because she might disapprove of or reject me.

15. The individual interests and qualities not shared by both of us in the beginning are now erased.

16. I am aware of saying phrases like, "we feel, we like, we think, we believe."

17. I focus on my partner's needs, wants, judgments, and reactions more than on my own.

18. My partner and I do everything together.

19. I feel as though I am losing my "self."

Purposeful Sexual Partnerships

The key word in this exercise is "purposeful." The purpose, however, is not to help your partner be the woman you thought she was. It is to accept your partner as she is.

That leaves the changing to you. You change yourself, not your partner. The purpose of this exercise is to notice the kind of partner you want to be in relationship with her.

"But I can't be the kind of partner I want to be until my partner is the kind of partner I need her to be."

This stance cheats you of being in charge of yourself. As an adult, you are every moment the individual and partner you want to be. You can be compassionate, rebellious, passive, or a combination, but you need neither permission nor approval to be you. Neither does your partner.

The next exercise offers another glimpse at how you can be more fully yourself as a partner. It's a chance to build your sexual relationship by developing to the point you really like who you are when you are with your partner.

The following statements have five options:

"never," "rarely," "sometimes," "frequently," or "always."

Choose one for each statement. You may dislike some of the statements, but it is important to discuss all of them. Be willing to observe your own behavior, hear your partner, and speak your truths compassionately.

Suggestions:

1. Fill out the exercise individually, then compare. Listen to your partner's response and to your answer for each item.

2. Note discrepancies. If you think you do something "always" and your partner says "never," you are on fertile ground. Note how you handle discrepancies and how you act or react together. Opportunity for increased sexual energy rests more in differentness than togetherness.

3. Note agreements. Appreciate them and move on; growth occurs slowly when people agree. Agreement promotes comfort and harmony, which should be obvious in your relationship.

4. Don't explode, don't cave in, and don't leave. Just quiet yourself.

5. When you have finished the exercise, discuss what it was like for you to talk about purposeful sexual partnership building.

Purposeful Sexual Partnerships

1. I actively listen when she wants to talk about sex even though I've heard it already.

   never   rarely   sometimes   frequently   always

2. My attitude is respectful even when I say "no."

   never   rarely   sometimes   frequently   always

3. I make appointments outside of bed to express sexual frustration.

   never   rarely   sometimes   frequently   always

4. I engage sexually with enthusiasm, fun, and laughter.

   never   rarely   sometimes   frequently   always

5. I make time for sex, just us, alone somewhere.

   never   rarely   sometimes   frequently   always

6. I criticize, withdraw, or get defensive after sex.

   never   rarely   sometimes   frequently   always

7. I stay present, clear, and handle my sexual anxiety.

   never   rarely   sometimes   frequently   always

8. During and after an argument about sex, I remain present until we get clear.

   never   rarely   sometimes   frequently   always

9. I feel connected to myself and my partner before, during, and after sex.

   never   rarely   sometimes   frequently   always

10. When she feels emotional, I am responsive.

    never   rarely   sometimes   frequently   always

11. When my partner gets on my nerves about sex, I want to discuss it.

    never   rarely   sometimes   frequently   always

12. We have outside interests and projects together.

    never   rarely   sometimes   frequently   always

13. One or both of us lives without sexual energy and wonder why it is absent.

    never   rarely   sometimes   frequently   always

Sexual Style

We don't think much about sexual style as a royal road to the unconscious; yet, your pattern of sexual style is a revealing form of subconscious communication. Your style is founded on subconscious script patterns that repeatedly block or support your sexuality. Although you might realize how your style blocks you from sexual enjoyment, you may not change because to do so can cause extreme anxiety, temporarily. Learning from temporary anxiety helps you manage and transform it into sexual energy.

Everyone has a sexual style even if they do not have a partner with whom to express it. Sexual style may or may not mimic personality style. For example, a passive, indecisive woman can be sexually assertive. A determined, dominant woman can be sexually shy, especially with a long-term partner. More often, styles follow the same patterns in and out of bed (or wherever you have sex). A chronically angry, suspicious woman is probably not a generous, sensitive lover. A chronically gentle, perceptive woman is probably not selfish and demanding in bed.

The few hours before partners have sex can reveal how a pattern begins and what happens next. A characteristic way of giving or receiving an invitation for sex might include being reserved, playful, enthusiastic, hesitant, funny, anxious, dominant, submissive, aggressive, passive, seductive, romantic, leading, following, expressive, self-confident, teasing, quiet, inviting, and so on. Other ways might include being hostile, mean, sadistic, masochistic, tricky, pitiful, fearful, guilty, selfish, etc.

The way you approach foreplay also reveals your sexual style and may suggest how you relate in other areas. For example, intrusion, shame, punishment, rejection, neglect, and fear of disapproval often inhibit or extinguish sexual desire and willingness to initiate. Expectations of pleasure and connection, or pain and distance, reveal an outlook about your relationship as much as about your sexuality. Expectations can reveal your patterns in other areas.

Foreplay is a subconscious, nonverbal interaction that directs what happens next. Examples of foreplay style include being giving, receptive, skilled, smooth, lusty, tentative, conventional, imaginative, persistent, reliable, conscientious, dramatic, leisurely, sensitive, assertive. Other styles might include being indifferent, self-absorbed, cautious, inhibited, aversive, distancing. Foreplay patterns are useful tools for change when you observe their effects. Foreplay, including the behaviors in which you no longer engage, hold a message about the meaning of sex to you. Foreplay and erotic behavior are not so much "skills" as they are physical communication of your desire for your partner.

Descriptions of orgasm style include being endearing, vigilant, lascivious, spontaneous, erotic, serious, primitive, tender, fun, adventurous, irreverent, loving, creative, juicy, insatiable, soulful. Some women use fantasy to trigger orgasms, a masturbatory experience during partner sex. Other styles might include being compliant, obligatory, dutiful, vigilant, intimidating, coercive, manipulative, abusive, disconnecting, distancing. An orgasm is not, after all, a measure of love, but an indication that your physical orgasmic arousal level has been reached.

People almost always find a partner whose sexual style can push their own sexual growth. Maturing partners find this delightful and fun rather than conflictual and disgusting, even when one is an incest survivor. For example, you might like vaginal penetration but your partner is turned off by it. You might want G-spot stimulation (see Suggested Reading, p. 107). The joy is being a competent adult experimenting with your competent adult partner. Emotional security does not require you to surrender your sense of self, compromise your integrity, or pretend helplessness when you are, in fact, capable. Even if nothing changes, pushing your sexual growth feels better than clinging to beliefs about safety and danger. The decision to enrich instead of comfort is difficult but necessary if you want to encourage healing and sexual intimacy.

For changing styles and patterns of behavior, *presence* is the most important ingredient. Partner sex without presence eventually becomes a masturbation experience and, hence, intolerable to a perceptive partner. Avoiding, spacing out, numbing, and emotional absence all distance you from your partner and, thus, prevent intimate sex. But when both partners need to push the other away to a comfortable distance, it becomes a conspicuous problem only when one begins to want more intimacy and less distance.

Suggestions:

1. Brainstorm with your partner to create a list of words that describe your respective sexual styles. Include every description you can think of.

2. In separate columns on the following page, note how you are similar and different. Talk about how these differences affect your respective sexual energy.

3. Create a map of an average sexual encounter or conversation about sex. The goal is to uncover a pattern and discuss how you might restructure or enhance it.

4. Don't explode, don't cave in, and don't leave. Just quiet yourself.

5. Discuss what it was like to talk about sexual style and the pattern yours reveals.

Notes

Sexual Style

Mine   Yours

Patterns of Sexual Behavior

(Use the characteristics you listed in "Sexual Style")

1. The first thing that happens is:

2. And then:

3. Here's how I predictably respond:

4. Here's how my partner predictably responds:

5. I do my predictable part because:

6. If I change my response, then:

7. I would change this if I:

Go back over your description and note which of your responses depend on your partner's behavior and which on your own. The secret to changing a pattern is to focus on yourself and be aware of your own options.

Maturity

Because the term "maturity" has a unique meaning to each of us, we invite you to design your own definition. Having a common definition of emotional maturity and knowing its meaning to your relationship moves you both in the direction of sexual fulfillment.

Here's how you can benefit from defining the term:

1. Maturity is the quality without which you will have a dull, unsexy, dependent relationship.

2. Maturity is vital to erotic sex because it helps you tolerate yearning for what you don't have, gives you courage to go for what you want, and offers freedom to accept or reject what others propose.

3. Maturity gives you the self-support to speak your truth, knowing it will push you both to contain and manage your reactions. You grow in self-respect each time you contain your urge to defend, criticize, cave in, or withdraw.

4. Maturity helps you avoid no-growth, no-change agreements and accept positive change.

5. Maturity gives you strength, options, and resources. It compels you to develop them in yourself instead of focusing on your partner's deficits. Awareness, courage, and maturity are requirements for erotic sex.

"Do you have to have a partner to develop maturity?"

No, but a partner will push your growth in almost every way you can imagine, and then some.

Our most efficient definition of maturity is: "Don't explode, don't cave in, and don't leave; just quiet yourself."

This means you contain but do not stifle your feelings as you listen actively to your partner. Containing your rebuttal lets you hear with intent, nonreactively, what she is saying. Control your impulses instead of letting your impulses control you. Set aside your rebuttal in favor of listening because you *want* to know her differentness. Arguing may be easier than listening and less threatening than being tender hearted, but it dulls sexual desire.

Suggestions:

1. Make time with your partner to read and discuss the statements on the next page. Add your personal favorites to the list. Discuss how you might develop greater maturity and what this might do to your relationship. Do not tell your partner how she should develop further. Focus on yourself, not on her.

2. Don't explode, don't cave in, and don't leave. Just quiet yourself.

3. When you have completed the exercise, talk about what it was like to define and discuss maturity.

Maturity is the ability to:

- Soothe your own anxiety, fear, discomfort, uneasiness, insecurities.

- Maintain your own identity in the face of pressure to conform to another's idea of how you should be.

- Tolerate your partner's intense emotions.

- Avoid protecting her from your intense feelings.

- Tolerate risk, ambivalence, and contradictions.

- Manage dissatisfaction and change.

- Stand apart as separate individuals while you value togetherness.

- Set your own limits with consideration for, not responsibility for, your partner.

- Respectfully share the best and worst of yourself.

- Look inside, tolerate what you see, and let each other in.

- Be of good will in words and action.

- Play together.

- Receive and give love and respect.

- Create balance in yourself when you are pulled off-center, and especially when you are wrong.

- Tolerate joy, grief, anger, fear, and orgasm.

Notes

Contradictions

Contradictions and paradoxes are normal, useful, everyday life events occurring both individually and between partners. A contradiction is an opposing, contrary, or conflicting opinion or event. A paradox is a statement or idea that is contrary to popular belief but that might actually be true. Both help you come to terms with differentness, separateness, and erotic energy.

Contradictions cause conflict and are useful for expanding your thinking. Managing contradiction is necessary for emotional growth. In a relationship, this means learning to synthesize conflicting ideas by bringing together seemingly opposite beliefs. To see contradiction from a higher vantage point, you view both sides of an argument as equally plausible and find a way to bring them into another, comprehensively different whole.

The statement, "I want my partner to want me, but I feel trapped by her" is a fertile contradiction that allows, or requires, self-observation. Is "being wanted" or "wanting" believable or even tolerable? Who imposes being "trapped?" Einstein said: "You cannot solve the problem on the level of the problem." This means you rise above the problem to see the whole picture. Then, you figure out that feeling trapped (and anything else) is a function of what you tell yourself, not a function of your partner's needs.

"I want an intimate relationship where I control what happens." In sexual relationships, intimacy happens between *peers*. One person does not control the other. Intimacy and emotional control do not exist side-by-side. Contradictions such as this one beg for clarity and higher thinking. Since you cannot have an intimate relationship by controlling, what can you have? You can have a parent-child relationship, but not a sexually intimate one.

Consciously accepting control of yourself removes you from a dependent position. Being accountable to yourself shifts you into genuineness. "I want an intimate relationship where I am in control of *me*," is a statement of authenticity and possibility. In relationship language, this means you value your perspective and her perspective whether you agree, disagree, or feel neutral. Creating "both and" instead of "either or" choices eliminates futile power struggles (do keep the useful ones) without erasing personal power.

Suggestions:

1. Read over the next exercise with your partner. Discover your own individual and interpersonal contradictions. Notice how easy or difficult it is for you to bring apparent opposites together. If one of you is quiet and the other expressive, you're on your way. Add your own thoughts to the list.

2. Don't explode, don't cave in, and don't leave. Just quiet yourself.

3. When you have finished the exercise, talk about what it was like to discuss your individual and interpersonal contradictions.

Using Contradictions

I Want...	And I also want...
To be close.	Solitude.
Self-reliance.	Dependability.
To love unconditionally.	To keep my love conditions.
To be loved and desired by my partner.	Bigger planetary concerns than the fact that I am desired.
To develop myself.	Growth to occur relationally.
Self-awareness and autonomy.	Suggestions and guidance.
To live in the moment.	To plan for the future.
Oneness with my partner.	Autonomy and individuality.
To work for harmony.	Some rest from this work.
Passion and intensity.	Friendship and reliability.
Sexual arousal & connection.	Companionship, peace,quiet.
To do all of this yesterday; life is too short to waste even one moment.	There is enough time for this; life is to be savored a little at a time.

Notes

Thoughts about Sex

Some thoughts about sex are easier to grasp than others. The next pages are an assortment of ideas shared by couples having sweeter and juicier sex the longer they are together. We apply their suggestions as we apply their collective guidelines to our own growing relationships.

Increasing your sexual intensity after "limerance" wears off happens as you experience the meaning of sex with your partner. Experiencing meaning is different from mental understanding. Meaning is something you attribute to your relationships: the one with yourself and the one with your partner. Talking about what sex means to each of you, what being with this particular woman means to you, giving meaning to everyday interactions, are discussions you can benefit from periodically, not just in the beginning.

Experience is more than understanding. It is being fully present with yourself while you are physically near your partner so that you "get" the connection deep in your bones. You know you've "got it," your partner knows, and you know she knows. Such profound knowing can be awkwardly uncomfortable and wonderfully intimate.

Experience supports presence as you grow in years. Age and experience deepen your sense of many personal issues and life events. Your values begin to shift as you gain autonomy and experience.

For example, thinking about performance is adolescent, yet, most of us do it. Worrying about performance suggests insecurity, not lovemaking. Requiring your partner's acceptance or reassurance will not help you feel erotic because your need focuses your attention on your partner, not on your experience. Thus, performance does not lead to erotic sex but to meeting

91

your need for reassurance. Your partner will eventually tire of the burden. Experience and autonomy let you know this.

On the other hand, playfulness and sensuality mixed with sexual contact, not reassurance or need, lends meaning through self-expression deeply felt with your beloved. That maturity allows playfulness without self-consciousness is, paradoxically, a gift from your child-self.

Suggestions:

1. Read the next page aloud with your partner. Make sense of the notions from your own relational perspectives. Add your own wisdom to the collection.

2. Don't explode, don't cave in, and don't leave. Just quiet yourself.

3. When you have finished what you can do for now, discuss what it was like for you to talk about the notions.

Thoughts about Sex

1. Unlike ordinary sex or sex in a state of mindless bliss, erotic sex is learned and developed over time.

2. You deepen your ability to love each time you see the other person clearly and accept who she is apart from your own needs and anxiety.

3. If you love yourself, you invite intimacy instead of attachment hunger into your life.

4. In a loving relationship you feel good about yourself most of the time, not bad.

5. Most women behave only as erotically as they believe their partner can tolerate.

6. Attention, compassion, conflict, and differentness are each powerful aphrodisiacs.

7. Communication, genital stimulation, skill, and arousal are necessary but not sufficient for erotic sex.

8. What is sufficient is the ability to balance high arousal with high anxiety and tip the scale in favor of arousal.

9. Compliant and obligatory sex lead to sexual apathy and resentment.

10. Sexual apathy is often an unspoken plea for presence, differentness, and autonomy.

11. No matter what the complaint, neither partner is innocent. Knowing this is vital to sex.

12. Until you can affirm yourself, your need for support prohibits your being fully erotic.

13. You must utilize considerable self-observation and self-support to be capable of erotic love.

14. Loving, wanting, and receiving require you to tolerate impermanence and loss.

15. Sexual exclusivity is a vow you make to yourself, not to your partner; it is a personal decision requiring maturity, self-respect, and a sense of fairness.

16. In a life partnership, one of you will eventually mourn the other. You can choose an intimate, erotic relationship, anyway, and suffer that loss but once, or suffer it a little each day that you choose comfort over intimacy.

With appreciation for personal communications over many years to Mary Goulding, and Drs. Joen Fagan, Kitty La Perriere, Thomas P. Malone, Natasha Mann, David M. Schnarch, Carl A. Whitaker, and Nisha Zenoff.

Sexual Potential

Sexual potential is the level to which you can aspire sexually. Undeveloped potential creates a "glass ceiling," the limit that keeps you from reaching your full capacity for sexuality. Pushing your underdeveloped sexuality toward its potential depends on your ability to soothe yourself, tolerate anxiety, manage pressure to conform, observe and use conflict and contradiction, and hold fast to your identity when pressed to be other than who you are. In other words, it is your level of maturity. Maturity in the form of emotional security requires you to acknowledge and accept yourself and your partner as you are now. The paradox is that before you can change and enrich yourself, you must first accept yourself.

You raise your sexual limit, your "glass ceiling" as you mature. If you have completed most of the handbook exercises, you have an idea of what maturity means to you and your partner. To approach your sexual potential, you first determine where and how your "glass ceiling" stops you from expressing yourself sexually. Fortunately, the "ceiling," your erotic energy cap, has nothing whatsoever to do with your partner. It is a figment of your own creation.

"Well, OK, but how does a person manage her own maturity and sexuality in a relationship?"

Caringly, not carefully. You affirm ownership of your own mind, body, and soul, including your desire to connect sexually with your partner. The "glass ceiling" is your challenge to claim every part of yourself, to use your inherent resources to change thoughts, feelings, and behaviors no longer useful to you, independent of your partner's patterns or responses. You then learn how to live with the resulting change, if any, in your partner.

Pushing your sexual relationship forward can feel risky. You have something to lose when you have energy invested in a relationship. Having little or no intimate energy for your partner minimizes your suffering when she leaves or dies. But, while you both live you are both deprived. Risking sexual feelings for your partner means the possibility for a loving, erotic relationship for the duration, however brief.

By approaching your sexual potential with integrity and maturity, you discover the experience that happens after you quiet yourself. You let your partner in, move your sexual energy forward and upward, sometimes together, right through the "ceiling." You can reinvent sacred sex in your own relationship, find that your "Dirty Goddess" energy makes you juicy and gives you joy and laughter. This is the real journey toward intimacy.

Suggestions:

1. Read the next page to yourself. If you think, "I could if only my partner would..." then focus on the part of your life for which you are independently responsible.

2. Don't explode, don't cave in, and don't leave. Just quiet yourself.

3. When you have finished, discuss what it was like to talk about your sexual potential.

Approaching Sexual Potential:

1. Willingness to be totally yourself, without pretense, including sexually.

2. The capacity to be caught off guard and enjoy the surprise and novelty.

3. The ability to find fresh possibilities in familiar surroundings.

4. The occasional longing for the presence and absence of your partner.

5. The ability to play, be sexually curious, be sexually creative.

6. Surrendering to the healing power of sexual intimacy for childhood and other wounds.

7. The ability to observe and manage your own anxiety, ambivalence, and contradictions.

8. The ability to tolerate your partner's anxiety, ambivalence, and contradictions.

9. Accepting life's unchangeable rhythms and cycles.

10. Accepting impermanence and loss, yet loving her anyway.

Notes

Practicing Loss

Nobody likes to do this last exercise; it is the most unfavorite. However, it is also the number one eye-opener for couples who can tolerate an erotically intimate relationship.

It is painful to anticipate the loss of your partner and relationship as you know it, unthinkable to speak about being alone after living with your familiar, beloved partner. Still, being mindful of life's inevitable endings can urge you toward planning your future, and more important, your present. The rewards are as sweet as the pain is going to be deep. You can decide at any time how you want to spend your remaining time together and how sweet it will be.

Practicing loss includes thinking about life without your partner. Death is inescapable, excusing you only in your wishful imagination, if you think of it at all. Denying death cheats you of living fully. You can plan for the eventuality of death or pretend to have unlimited time. Either way has consequences. Although planning for eventual loss is painful, it can make the present precious and sweet. Valuing your partner and your time together, and planning an inevitable future, are developmental tasks whatever your age and however much time you *think* you have left.

If you are over fifty, think about the next decades and how you want to spend them with your partner. Think about growing old together and what that means to you. Then think about growing old alone, how you might manage emotionally and socially. Will you move forward in your own living and loving? How will you survive the tragedy of your loss?

If you are under fifty, think about what the next years might bring if your partner were to die prematurely. Think about being alone and how you might manage emotionally, socially, and yes, financially. Will you move forward in your own living and loving? How will you survive the tragedy of your loss?

The tragedy of love is that its partner is death. The gift of life is going after what you want, now, not despite that but because of it. One might say that life is foreplay for death.

Suggestions:

1. Read the next page alone, and then do the exercise.

2. Later, read to each other what you have written.

3. Talk about what losing your partner means to you.

4. Discuss responses to your own experience of planning for loss.

5. Don't explode, don't cave in, and don't leave. Just quiet yourself.

6. When you have finished, discuss what it was like to talk about practicing loss.

Practicing Loss

1. Bring together your thoughts about your partner and what losing her means to you. Write that, here.

2. Write your partner's epitaph: a few words for her gravestone that express your thoughts about her.

3. Write a short love note to your alive partner. Include appreciations, resentments, and regrets, in that order about your time together until now.

Notes

Closing Comments

Several thousand years ago, before the shift to patriarchy, sexuality was a sacred celebration. Reclaiming that same sense of sacredness is an intuitive, redevelopmental task for today's women. You can begin reopening this divine realm by exploring the blessings in your own relationship. When connecting with your partner stirs your soul, use that bonding toward soulful communion. Uncover the sacred meaning of your own sexual energy.

Many, if not all, intimate moments are sacred. Sharing these moments with words is often impossible, yet couples report spiritual bonding that happens through nonverbal vocabularies of love, such as silence, music, dance, art, nature, and even work, for some. Connecting to a higher power, and through that higher power connecting with your beloved or, conversely, finding a higher power through physical contact with your beloved can and does happen. A simultaneous deep connection to yourself, your partner, and a higher power *is* sacred energy. Please find your way, and let us know about your process.

Sacred pleasure, the spiritual aspect of connecting with your beloved through erotic sex, is deliberately not addressed in this handbook. Nonetheless, the sacred meaning to your sexual energy awaits your discovery.

Finding a way to unite your higher selves, for example, through Tantra, is described by Margot Anand in *The Art of Sexual Ecstacy* (see Suggested Readings, p. 107). Tantra is an ancient Eastern process of spirituality expressed physically. Tantric sex encourages you toward sacred, blissful moments and is worth exploring with your partner. It will be most useful after you have learned to manage your anxiety and soothe yourself.

Sex "how-to" books are available for learning technical skills, and some are quite useful, especially those by JoAnn Loulan and Celeste West (see Suggested reading, p. 107).

May the rest of your journey proceed with love, laughter, integrity, and sacred feminine mysteries to guide you through a life lived gloriously together.

Appendix

Toning Your Orgasm Muscles

Toning the orgasm muscles enhance orgasms. Women have exercised their orgasm (pubococcygeal or "PC") muscles for centuries. In 1940 Dr. Arnold Kegel got credit for describing them in a medical journal, prescribing them for incontinent patients to help them hold urine. Not only did patients report better urinary control, they said their orgasms got stronger or happened for the first time!

People who exercise their PC muscles often report stronger orgasms. This is particularly true for women over thirty-five and of any age who have given birth. People lose PC muscle tone with age, so exercising will help regain it. After you build tone with daily practice, a maintenance schedule of three times a week will keep you toned, depending on your age and health. PC exercises can be practiced anywhere at almost any time (except while driving or operating any kind of equipment that requires your full attention).

To identify your PC muscles, imagine sitting on the toilet with your knees spread comfortably apart. Release and stop an imaginary flow of urine. PC muscles are the only muscles able to stop urine flow in this position. When you recognize your PC muscles, you can practice unobserved in any position: prone, sitting, standing, or walking. The only giveaway is the look on your face if you trigger an orgasm!

PC exercises should be done briefly, one to six times a day, divided into no more than five minutes at a time, and no more than fifteen minutes total in any one day. Beginners should start with one minute or less and build gradually to five minutes over several weeks. Remember to stop or rest when muscles tire. This exercise is to build and enhance pleasure, not endurance.

Like any other muscle, the PC gets painfully sore with too much exercise. Your goal is not to overexercise but rather to build muscle tone very slowly, preferably over four to six weeks. If muscles get sore, cut the exercises back by at least 75%. Check with your physician if soreness persists.

Exercise I: Contract and relax your PC muscles rapidly (not intensely). Begin with ten or fifteen brief, gentle contractions, build to twenty-five during the first week, fifty the second, seventy-five the third, until you can do about 150 at the end of a month or two. When you build to fifty, add Exercise II.

Exercise II: Contract your PC muscles, hold in for four to eight seconds, then relax. Begin with five contractions and gradually, slowly, build to about fifty. When you can do fifty, add Exercise III.

Exercise III: Imagine a ping pong ball rests at the opening of your vagina. Tighten your PC muscles as if to suck the ball slowly and deeply into your vaginal opening. Begin with about five strong "pulls" and build to about fifty or whatever number feels right.

Suggested Readings

Anand, Margo. (1989). *The Art of Sexual Ecstasy: The Path of Sacred Sexuality for Western Lovers.* Los Angeles: Jeremy P. Tarcher, Inc.

Berzon, Betty. (1988). *Permanent Partners: Building gay and Lesbian relationships that last.* NY: E. P. Dutton.

Berzon, Betty. (1996). *The Intimacy Dance: A Guide to Long Term Success in Gay and Lesbian Relationships.* NY: E. P. Dutton.

Califia, Pat. (1988). *Sapphistry: The Book Of Lesbian Sexuality.* Tallahassee, FL: Naiad.

Caster, Wendy. (1993). *The Lesbian Sex Book.* Los Angeles: Alyson.

Dodson, Betty. (1987). *Sex for One: The Joy of Selfloving.* NY: Harmony Books.

Gottman, John. (1995). *Why Marriages Succeed or Fail.* NY: Simon & Schuster.

Johnson, Susan E. (1990). *Staying Power: Long Term Lesbian Couples.* Tallahassee, FL: Naiad.

Ladas, Alice, Whipple, Beverly, & Perry, John. (1983). *The G Spot.* NY: Dell.

Loulan, Jo Ann. (1984). *Lesbian Sex.* Spinsters Ink: San Francisco.

Loulan, Jo Ann. (1987). *Lesbian Passion: Loving ourselves and each other.* San Francisco: Spinsters/Aunt Lute.

Loulan, Jo Ann. (1990). *The Lesbian Erotic Dance: Butch, Femme, Androgyny and Other Rhythms*. Spinsters: San Francisco.

McDaniel, Judith. (1995). *The Lesbian Couples Guide: Finding the right woman and creating a life together*. NY: Harper Collins.

Malone, Thomas P., & Malone, Patrick T. (1987). *The Art of Intimacy*. NY: Prentiss Hall.

Malone, Patrick T., & Malone, Thomas P. (1992). *The Windows of Experience*. NY: Simon & Schuster.

Morganthaler, John, & Joy, Dan. (1994). *Better Sex Through Chemistry*. Petaluma, CA: Smart Publications.

Schnarch, David. (1997). *Passionate Marriage: Sex, love, & intimacy in emotionally committed relationships*. NY: W. W. Norton.

Tieffer, Leonore. (1995). *Sex Is Not A Natural Act and Other Essays*. Boulder: Westview.

West, Celeste. (1989). *A Lesbian Love Advisor*. Pittsburgh: Cleis Press.

West, Celeste. (1997). *Lesbian Polyfidelity*. San Francisco: Booklegger.

Community Resources

American Academy of Psychotherapists (AAP)
P.O. Box 611
New Bern, NC 28563

Phone: 919-634-3066   Fax: 919-634-3067
E-mail: aapoffice@aol.com

American Association of Marriage and Family Therapists
(AAMFT)
10th floor
1100 17th Street NW
Washington, DC 20036

Phone: 202-452-0109   Fax: 202-223-2329
Web access: www.aamft.org

American Association of Sex Educators, Counselors, and
Therapists (AASECT)
P.O. Box 238
Mount Vernon, IA 52314

Phone: 319-895-8407   Fax: 319-895-6203

The Society for the Scientific Study of Sexuality
P.O. Box 208
Mount Vernon, IA 52314

Phone: 319-895-8407   Fax: 319-895-6203

Sexuality Information and Education Council of the U. S. (SIECUS)
University of Pennsylvania
Graduate School of Education
3700 Walnut Street
Philadelphia, PA 19104-6216

Web access: http://www.siecus.org

Your State Psychological Association, Nurses Ass'n, Social Workers Ass'n, Marriage and Family Therapists Ass'n, Licensed Professional Counselors Ass'n (Blue Pages in telephone book).

Your State Licensure Board

The above national and local organizations can refer you to qualified couples/sexual therapists in your area, should you want a consultation. Please be certain any therapist you consider has credentials *from your state Licensure Board*. Credentials from AAMFT and AASECT indicate expertise over and above a license to practice.

About the Authors

Virginia Erhardt, Ph.D., is a licensed psychologist and sex therapist in independent practice in the Atlanta area. She is creator of the *Autonomy and Intimacy* seminars for single lesbians, co-creator of the *Maturity and Passion* workshops for lesbian couples, and co-creator of the weekend *Retreat for Lesbian Couples*. She writes a column for *Southern Voice*, the weekly gay newspaper for the southeast. Since 1988, she has led workshops and offered trainings on relationships, sexuality, gender identity, and sexual orientation issues. Her grandchildren and her partner of 18 years brighten her life and the planet.

Jeanne Shaw, Ph.D., is a licensed psychologist, clinical nurse specialist, AASECT certified sex therapist, and Clinical Director of the Couples Enrichment Institute of Atlanta, Georgia. She developed the *Retreat for Couples* weekend sexuality workshop, and co-designed the *Maturity and Passion* and *Retreat for Lesbian Couples* weekends. Author of dozens of professional articles, she has led Sexual Attitude Reassessment programs and other sexual enrichment workshops and training seminars in this country and abroad since 1973. Currently, she is writing a book about age and sexual potential and enjoying an increasing crop of grandchildren in the U.S. and Israel.

The authors have researched, presented, and published twenty years of work focused on the relationships of sexual individuals and couples. Their work has been reported to numerous professional and scientific organizations.

Evaluation

Journey Toward Intimacy for Partner #1

Female, Age_____

Length of partnership_____

1. Please indicate your purposes in using this workbook (check all that apply):

____ A. To help me explore personal questions or concerns.
____ B. To find deeper relatedness with my partner.
____ C. To satisfy my curiosity.
____ D. Because my teacher, friend, spouse, therapist recommended it (circle all that apply).
____ E. To update my knowledge for relationships, work, school, career (circle all that apply).
____ F. Other:

2. Was the workbook personally beneficial?

____ A. Not at all, a waste of time and money.
____ B. Slightly, I got a little bit but not much.
____ C. Moderately, it was good in some places.
____ D. Very much, I got a lot from doing it.
____ E. Greatly, I had a transformative experience.

3. Did you complete all of the exercises, including discussions?
☐ Yes   ☐ No

4. Did you talk about what it was like to discuss each topic after each exercise?   ☐ Yes ☐ No

5. Which exercises were most valuable for you? How?

6. Which exercises were least valuable for you? How?

7. What changes would you suggest?

8. Are you interested in other sexuality workbooks?

_____ A. Men's
_____ B. Midlife
_____ C. Over 65
_____ D. Heterosexual couples
_____ E. Physical disabilities or medical problems

Other comments?

Thank you for taking the time to give feedback. Your response to this survey will help ongoing research.

Please return this form to:
Couples Enrichment Institute
P.O. Box 420114
Atlanta, GA 30342-0114

Evaluation

Journey Toward Intimacy for Partner #2

Female, Age_____

Length of partnership_____

1. Please indicate your purpose(s) in using this workbook (check all that apply):

____ A. To help me explore personal questions or concerns.
____ B. To find deeper relatedness with my partner.
____ C. To satisfy my curiosity.
____ D. Because my teacher, friend, spouse, therapist recommended it (circle all that apply).
____ E. To update my knowledge for relationships, work, school, career (circle all that apply).
____ F. Other:

2. Was the workbook personally beneficial?

____ A. Not at all, a waste of time and money.
____ B. Slightly, I got a little bit but not much.
____ C. Moderately, it was good in some places.
____ D. Very much, I got a lot from doing it.
____ E. Greatly, I had a transformative experience.

3. Did you complete all of the exercises, including discussions?
   ☐ Yes   ☐ No

4. Did you talk about what it was like to discuss each topic after each exercise?   ☐ Yes   ☐ No

5. Which exercises were most valuable for you? How?

6. Which exercises were least valuable for you? How?

7. What changes would you suggest?

8. Are you interested in other sexuality workbooks?

____ A. Men's
____ B. Midlife
____ C. Over 65
____ D. Heterosexual couples
____ E. Physical disabilities or medical problems

Other comments?

Thank you for taking the time to give feedback. Your response to this survey contributes to ongoing research.

Please return this form to:
Couples Enrichment Institute
P.O. Box 420114
Atlanta, GA 30342-0114

Retreat for Lesbian Couples: A Weekend Workshop

Some of the exercises in this handbook are used in the **Journey Toward Intimacy: Retreat for Lesbian Couples**, known previously as Maturity and Passion workshops. The Retreat is held in a quiet setting near Atlanta. The format includes mini-lectures, verbal and written exercises between partners, group discussion, and time for play.

The unique format helps couples, including sexual abuse survivors and their partners, to move forward with respect and awareness for their own pace, without being re-traumatized. Like the handbook, the purpose of the weekend experience is to embrace a perspective about lesbian sexuality that encourages self-respect, integrity, and intimate sexual energy between life partners.

If you and your partner would like a quiet, structured weekend away from home to reconnect and learn more about yourself and each other and, please contact:

virgpsych@aol.com

or

Write for a brochure:

Virginia Erhardt, Ph.D.
1924 Clairmont Road, Suite 120
Decatur, GA 30033

Don't Explode
Don't Cave In
Don't Leave

Quiet Yourself

Couples Enrichment Institute
P. O. Box 420114, Atlanta, GA 30342-0114

ORDER FORM

Fax orders: (404) 255-7439

Online orders: forcouples@mindspring.com

Postal orders: Couples Enrichment Institute
P.O. Box 420114
Atlanta, GA 30342-0114, USA

Visit our website at http://www.mindspring.com/~forcouples/index.html

Qty	*Journey Toward Intimacy*	Unit	Total
	A Handbook for Couples	$12.99	
	A Handbook for Lesbian Couples	$12.99	
	A Handbook for Gay Couples	$12.99	
	A Handbook for Singles	$12.99	
$2.00 shipping for first book and $.50 per book thereafter			
Total			

Payment enclosed:

☐ Check (amount in U.S. dollars): $ _____

☐ _____   ____/____
    VISA or Mastercard Number   Expiration

Signature: _____

Print Name: _____

Shipping address: _____
                Street   Apt. No.

_____
City   State   Zip

I understand I may return any unused, resalable books for a complete refund.

ORDER FORM

Fax orders: (404) 255-7439

Online orders: forcouples@mindspring.com

Postal orders: Couples Enrichment Institute
                   P.O. Box 420114
                   Atlanta, GA 30342-0114, USA

Visit our website at http://www.mindspring.com/~forcouples/index.html

Qty	*Journey Toward Intimacy*	Unit	Total
	A Handbook for Couples	$12.99	
	A Handbook for Lesbian Couples	$12.99	
	A Handbook for Gay Couples	$12.99	
	A Handbook for Singles	$12.99	
$2.00 shipping for first book and $.50 per book thereafter			
Total			

Payment enclosed:

☐ Check (amount in U.S. dollars): $ _____

☐ _____   ____ /____
    VISA or Mastercard Number   Expiration

Signature: _____

Print Name: _____

Shipping address: _____
                       Street   Apt. No.

_____
City   State   Zip

I understand I may return any unused, resalable books for a complete refund.

ORDER FORM

Fax orders: (404) 255-7439

Online orders: forcouples@mindspring.com

Postal orders: Couples Enrichment Institute
P.O. Box 420114
Atlanta, GA 30342-0114, USA

Visit our website at http://www.mindspring.com/~forcouples/index.html

Qty	*Journey Toward Intimacy*	Unit	Total
	A Handbook for Couples	$12.99	
	A Handbook for Lesbian Couples	$12.99	
	A Handbook for Gay Couples	$12.99	
	A Handbook for Singles	$12.99	
$2.00 shipping for first book and $.50 per book thereafter			
Total			

Payment enclosed:

☐ Check (amount in U.S. dollars): $_____

☐ _____ ____/____
     VISA or Mastercard Number   Expiration

Signature: _____

Print Name: _____

Shipping address: _____
                Street   Apt. No.

_____
City   State   Zip

I understand I may return any unused, resalable books for a complete refund.

ORDER FORM

Fax orders: (404) 255-7439

Online orders: forcouples@mindspring.com

Postal orders: Couples Enrichment Institute
                  P.O. Box 420114
                  Atlanta, GA 30342-0114, USA

Visit our website at http://www.mindspring.com/~forcouples/index.html

Qty	*Journey Toward Intimacy*	Unit	Total
	A Handbook for Couples	$12.99	
	A Handbook for Lesbian Couples	$12.99	
	A Handbook for Gay Couples	$12.99	
	A Handbook for Singles	$12.99	
$2.00 shipping for first book and $.50 per book thereafter			
Total			

Payment enclosed:

☐ Check (amount in U.S. dollars): $_____

☐ _____   ____/____

    VISA or Mastercard Number   Expiration

Signature: _____

Print Name: _____

Shipping address: _____
                  Street   Apt. No.

_____
City   State   Zip

I understand I may return any unused, resalable books for a complete refund.